UNAPPRECIATED TO UNSTOPPABLE

Break Free from Thankless Situations as
You Embrace Empowerment, Joy and Authenticity

AARTI MEHTA-NAYYAR

Unappreciated to Unstoppable
Copyright © 2025 by Aarti Mehta-Nayyar.
All rights reserved.

No part of this book may be reproduced, stored in a retrieval system, or transmitted in any form or by any means—electronic, mechanical, photocopying, recording, or otherwise—without the prior written permission of the publisher, except in the case of brief quotations embodied in reviews and certain other noncommercial uses permitted by copyright law.

Printed in the United States of America.
ISBN: 978-1-958165-46-1 (Paperback)
ISBN: 978-1-958165-43-0 (Hardback)
ISBN: 978-1-958165-44-7 (eBook)

FOREWORD

THERE ARE SOME rare people I have met on this planet who, simply by being themselves, light up the lives of everyone around them. Aarti is one of those rare souls. As her friend, I have witnessed her journey—a path not only of resilience but of unshakeable warmth and boundless strength. Her story is one of transformation, from quietly striving for external validation to boldly embracing her power, a journey that has given her a rare and beautiful clarity about life.

In Unappreciated to Unstoppable, Aarti opens her heart with profound generosity. She shares her journey, not just as a mother and a coach, but as a friend who understands the challenges of self-doubt, and as a guide who's walked through them to find her way to peace and self-approval. With gentle wisdom, she reminds us that true empowerment doesn't come from applause or external recognition but from within.

This book is more than a guide; it's a gift for anyone who's ever felt overlooked, undervalued, or unsure of their worth. Aarti's voice is gentle, yet powerful, encouraging readers to stop seeking approval in others' eyes and instead look inside their own hearts. Her message is deeply relatable because she has lived it herself, and she offers a roadmap that feels warm, kind, and, most importantly, REAL.

As you turn these pages, let Aarti's words remind you that the journey to becoming unstoppable starts with self-love and self-trust. Thank you, Aarti, for leading us with your light!

Francesca Facio Crespo, Writer, Coach & International Speaker

CONTENTS

Foreword iii
Dedication vii
Introduction ix
    How to Best Use This Book xv
    What is Validation? xviii

Section 1: Rediscover Yourself 1
    Chapter 1: Know Yourself 3
    Chapter 2: Know That You Are Enough 11
    Chapter 3: Self-awareness 19

Section 2: Reclaim Your Space 29
    Chapter 4: Adjust Your Hindsight Window 31
    Chapter 5: Be Your Own Cheerleader 41
    Chapter 6: Compassion and Forgiveness 51
    Chapter 7: Redesign Your Reality 63

Section 3: Build Your Spiritual Armor 73
    Chapter 8: Set Boundaries 75
    Chapter 9: Recharge Your Batteries 85

Chapter 10: Understand Your Triggers and
    Be Prepared 95
Chapter 11: Build Your Community 103

Unstoppable YOU 111
Glossary 115
About the Author 121

DEDICATION

*To my parents who continue to teach me to
BE: kind, compassionate, and loving.*

*To my daughters Uma and Aarya who inspire me
to BE: curious, playful, and unapologetic.*

*To my husband Nakul who supports me in my
BEing: creative, growing, and ever evolving.*

*To you dear reader for your commitment to
BE: your true, authentic, empowered self.*

INTRODUCTION

wear my father's old shirts, love with all my heart, and live with all my soul.

My love and respect for my family and for my family's generational values were constantly questioned by the cultural entities around me. It was assumed that if I didn't follow the norm, I wasn't a good human. I needed fixing, and my parents were shown compassion for putting up with an outlier like me.

So if I were living my life on my terms and breaking and challenging norms, then why as a 40+ year old woman did I suddenly find myself at a point where despite having it all—a supportive husband, amazing kids, parents in good health, an amazing connection with my brother, friends that each day showed me that friendships are limitless, an amazing home, and a wonderful job—why then did I feel disillusioned? Why did I not feel truly happy, that silly happy that I once was capable of? As I tried to find the answer to this, I realized something.

Although I had started my journey breaking rules and challenging norms, somewhere along the way, I started looking outwards for reference, for approval. I wanted to really be the best in my new roles, that of a daughter-in-law, a wife and a mother, and as I began to look outwards, I got caught in the trap of seeking external validation. I started changing, and unfortunately, it wasn't for the better.

As it happens, when you look outwards, you are faced by the demands put forth by your society and/or your culture.

In my case, it demanded that I be quiet and accept anything someone older than me said, right or wrong; I was told this was a sign of respect.

It demanded that I put everyone else first, that it was a sign of love.

It demanded that I follow the roadmap laid out for the various roles I have—daughter, wife, daughter-in-law, mother—as it was a sign of being responsible.

It demanded that I love and invite into my home even those who harshly judged, criticized, or even disrespected me; it was a sign of family values.

I was now trying to be "honorable, responsible, and demonstrative of my family values."

I started caring what everyone else thought, and I started getting judged on everything to do with me. I received "reviews" about everything—my work, my house keeping skills, my cooking skills, my skills as a mother, my post-pregnancy weight, absolutely anything and everything associated with me. And the painful part about reviews is that not all of them are kind and encouraging. In my case, if on a rare occasion the reviews were kind, they didn't ring true because I had lost touch with my soul.

As I got bogged down by the harsh judgments, the unkind words, and the criticisms, I got tired, drained, exhausted, and critical of myself. The more criticism I faced, the more I tried to please and seek validation, and

INTRODUCTION

the more I sought validation, the more I got criticized, and that's how I got stuck in a negative spiral that led to a period of self-doubt. This self-doubt spread its vicious tentacles in other aspects of my life as well. These were areas where I was previously most confident like my work life, my worth as a friend, as a sister, a daughter, and even as a human.

Lucky for me, there came a point where it got too much for me, unbearable even, and I was driven to seek a better solution. Hence, from this period of self-doubt, I embarked on my journey of self-discovery. I started reconnecting with my inner self, my true self, my essence, and my spirit.

In this search, I constantly came across the notion that suggested that if I was stuck in a pattern, this was actually the universe trying to send me a message and teach me a key lesson. I pondered on these words and wondered, if I am doing everything to be a good person and if people around me continue to be unkind to me, what could possibly be the lesson for me here?

But as I broke out of my victim persona (where I felt that life was happening to me and I had no control) and tried to truly understand the message in my experiences and began to seek answers, I realized that the universe wanted me to learn to live a fully expressed life. It wanted me to be ME. It wanted me to follow my own soul print (that calling that would make my heart sing with joy and enable me to live a life aligned with my values, where I will be as excited about the journey as the destination).

I began to realize I was being measured on a set of goals that weren't even mine. I learned that as much as I was in awe of supermodels, it was never my goal to be one, what I wanted was a healthy body. I learned that as much as I was inspired by great cooks around me, it wasn't my goal to become a chef; what I wanted was to cook simple and nutritious food for my family and me. I realized that as impressive as it was for me to see all the full-time moms and dedicated homemakers around me, it wasn't my goal to be one. What I wanted was to give my family a loving and comforting space while giving myself the space to follow my dreams and also be financially independent.

I learned that my life's purpose, my goal was that I wanted to be a light in this world, my spirit wanted to touch lives and make people happier, and every moment of self-doubt and self-criticism took me further away from my spiritual goal.

That is when I realized the interesting thing about approval. The only approval that really matters in our life is our own. Approval or disapproval of others is a mere reflection of their own journey and their respective values and/or insecurities.

As I started working from the place of my core values and with alignment to my true spirit, I realized it was easy for me to feel validated by myself and it was that self-validation that fueled me, energized me to feel happier and to feel more fulfilled with each passing day!

INTRODUCTION

I started noticing more and more people around me who were struggling with the same demons that I had now conquered. I was inspired to follow my soul print and I trained to become a life coach so that I could help relieve others of the apathy that I once suffered from. To fulfill this goal, I have designed a framework that can help others achieve internal validation.

It is my mission to make this journey to self-validation and freedom from criticism available to everyone.

It is important to me that more and more people experience self-validation and break free from the shackles of external approval so that more and more people experience bliss, joy, and happiness and are propelled to start following their dreams, their soul print and live to their fullest potential.

How to Best Use This Book

Before you begin to read this book, I invite you to take a pause. This book may have been recommended to you; it may have been gifted to you or you may have picked it out of curiosity. Regardless of how it happened in your life, I invite you to pause and think of what urged you to turn the page and begin reading. Because it is in that instance that you consciously or subconsciously decided that you want to explore the concept of self-validation further.

So take a pause and write your thoughts below.

Where and when do you feel most judged? How does that make you feel? Which area of your life do you have feelings of self-doubt and unworthiness?

Why this book and what do you hope to get from this book?

_____

_____

_____

_____

_____

_____

_____

INTRODUCTION

Now that you know what you want to achieve from this commitment, I would like to explain the best way to get value from this book. This book is not for the passive reader.

To gain the most value and the best outcome for yourself, commit yourself to each exercise. Try not to rush through this book. Take a couple of days to a week for each chapter, but do not go more than a week between chapters.

For you to leverage this book the most, I invite you to head over to my web-site, www.coachAarti.com, here you will find additional material to support you in your journey.

Remember, you get what you put in; you picked this book because you recognized that in one or more areas of your life, you are not fully expressed and you don't feel the approval. This is your first step; are you ready to commit?

- ☐ YES

- ☐ YES, I was born ready for this

- ☐ HELL YES, I can't wait to unleash my power!!!

I would also like to remind you that breaking out of the pattern that you have potentially followed for years, if not decades, takes time, love, and patience. Please give yourself grace, come back to this book as many times as you need, because each time it will unlock something new for you!

I hope in this book and in me, you find a confidant and cheerleader for your self-validation journey.

INTRODUCTION

WHAT IS VALIDATION?

Before we get started, let's understand a few key concepts that form the basis of what we will be working on.

It is important to remember, there are two types of Validation—Internal and External. This chapter is written with the lens of external validation. Internal validation, which is a more positive space to be in, and what we will be working toward, will be discussed in future chapters.

Validation: A quick Google search got me to—among others—the following very apt definition of Validation -> recognition or affirmation that a person or their feelings or opinions are valid or worthwhile.

I love this definition because in this simple statement, you read that validation is a complete submission of your thoughts and actions for discernment.

When you submit to another human, you experience external validation. This validation does not take you into account. It is simply you being judged by another individual who has no understanding of your core, your values, your circumstances, or challenges. This is the reason why external validation doesn't usually resonate with us. This is why it feels empty when it is positive and why it hurts when it's negative. Most of all, this is the reason why this quest for external validation is a pointless pursuit. We become mere people-pleasers and disconnect from ourselves as we seek external validation.

The person whom you have now given the power to approve of your actions or behaviors does not share your past experiences or your future goals and desires. They do not have the same present as you nor the same moral values as you. They do not have the same interests, passions, likes, or dislikes as you. They do not think like you, behave like you or act like you, and yet you have given them the power to judge you. In addition, you now take that judgment at face value and let it become the measure of your worthiness.

In contrast, when you submit to yourself, you experience internal validation, which is your ability to affirm based on your own values, your circumstances, and your life vision/goals. You experience self-validation as you acknowledge your growth and transformations with your unique experiences and constraints.

If seeking validation is so painful, why do we keep doing it?

As a species, and as part of our evolution, one of the most critical aspects in our human history that ensured our survival was the sense of belonging. We needed to belong to and be accepted by our family/community/tribe for our growth and survival. This need for belonging is what drove us to make sure we adhered to the rules laid by the tribe that we were seeking to be part of. To get further assurance of our space and security within the tribe, we started looking for cues that suggested we were wanted. That is where the need for validation came in.

INTRODUCTION

As we have moved on from surviving to thriving, our needs have evolved and the need for us, now, is to belong to a tribe of like-minded people with the same values, goals, and visions as us. And luckily for us, we are at a time and age when we can choose the tribe we want to be part of; the world is our oyster and we no longer need to limit ourselves geographically to find our tribe. You can start today by joining our tribe of validation breakers, details at www.coachAarti.com.

So what are the impacts of constantly seeking validation?

While the impacts are many, I will only list a few. My intent here is not to have you delve too much on the negative, rather just understand what could be at stake here.

- You lose yourself - This to me is perhaps the most painful outcome of a validation-seeking behavior. Over time, all your actions are molded by a sense of what another person is looking for. What would they like? What would bring a nod of approval, a look of respect, a word of kindness as a reaction to the work you are doing. You are so driven by this end goal and desire that you soon forget who you are and what your own way of discerning certain actions might be. You begin to feel dispirited.

- You lose your sense of worthiness - As you follow this nearly unattainable goal of external validation, you lose your sense of worth. You begin to forget your strengths and accept your challenges. You forget that we all here are imperfect beings meant to constantly grow and evolve and you are no different. You forget the flawsome, wonderful being that you are.

- You feel drained and start thinking of life as a rut, you hope to achieve happiness at a future time. When you live a Iife constantly striving for approval, you are drained; the job to please others is never done because there are as many opinions as there are people in this world. The pursuit for everyone's approval tires you out and you feel exhausted and fatigued throughout the day. You hope that at some point in the future, you will be able to experience the bliss, joy, and happiness you are craving.

- You disconnect from your soul purpose - We all get to enjoy this human experience while working toward a sense of satisfaction, calm, and joy (our soul purpose) however, as we start seeking external validation, we disconnect from this purpose. We forget our special gifts, the dreams we dreamed as kids, the desires that burnt through us as youth. We become puppets living our life to someone else's tune.

Validation Exercise

How do I know that I am stuck in a validation-seeking spiral?

Answer the following questions with a simple Yes/No.

- When you achieve something, rather than enjoy the sweet satisfaction of successfully meeting your goal, is your first thought that you need to share this achievement with someone else to see if they like it? Are you not sure that you have been successful and are waiting for someone else to confirm it for you?

- When someone does acknowledge you for an achievement, can you take it at face value, or do you feel they are just being polite or dishonest with you?

- If you have done something for someone, are you constantly trying to read them to see if they like it or not? Example: cooking food, throwing a party, getting a gift.

- Are you constantly shrinking yourself? Example: getting less vocal about your likes and dislikes.

- Do you feel like you have no time for yourself? Are you constantly meeting everyone's priorities at the cost of your own? Do you feel you don't have the time to indulge in your own pleasures, reading, writing, painting, music, dancing, self-care, exercise?

- Do you feel that no one notices the impact you have on their life, that they do not value you enough?

- Do you feel that at present you have no time for your goals and dreams? That they have either been forgotten in your past or have been placed on hold for a future time?

If you answered Yes to three or more of the questions, you might be putting too much emphasis on seeking external validation.

Section 1

REDISCOVER YOURSELF

The answer lies within, it always has!
In this section, we will peel away the layers, we will lovingly let go of that which is not part of our authentic expression, we will get to know ourselves on a deeper level and experience a beautiful reunion with our soul.

CHAPTER 1

Know Yourself

Don't let your special character and values, the secret that you know and no one else does, the truth - don't let that get swallowed up by the great chewing complacency.
—Aesop

DO YOU FEEL you truly know yourself, or are you so busy living life on others' terms that you barely take pause to reflect on your values and live a life that's truly authentic?

There is a beautiful story I heard: There was a river that was swelling with the recent rains, and as the water gushed past, it washed away anything that lay in its path. As the villagers watched the rapids, a monk among them noticed a scorpion being washed into the water. The monk quickly jumped into the water, scooped out the scorpion and put it on a rock. As soon as the scorpion was out of danger, it stung the monk. The villagers saw this and explained to the monk that scorpions sting, and that's why everyone keeps a safe distance from them.

After a few minutes, the scorpion again got washed into the water. The monk once again went to scoop it out, only to be stung once again. All the villagers laughed; they felt this wise monk was not that wise after all. They had much more wisdom than a monk. A villager asked the monk, "If you know the scorpion stings, why do you keep repeating your mistake and rescuing it?" The monk replied, "Because it is the scorpion's nature to sting and mine to save. It is true to its nature and I am true to mine!"

I find this story wonderful. In my opinion, this story demonstrates beautifully why it is important for you to be aware and aligned with your values. The monk was not impacted by the judgment and ridicule of others because he knew undoubtedly what his core values were, and despite being mocked, he knew he was operating from a place of being true to himself.

As I was adapting to society's expectations of fulfilling my roles, I was losing my connection to myself. The divide between how I truly wanted to show up in life and how I was showing up in life began to grow bigger and bigger. I could no longer see the shore as I began to lose myself and started feeling like a rudderless ship. In still waters, I was able to get by, but the moment I faced choppy waters in terms of challenges in my life, I would spiral out of control and even small challenges seemed tough to face and overcome.

If you are not living your values, I guarantee you, that the person you are today is a mere shadow of who you once were and/or who you are meant to be. As you grow up, you start thinking that life is serious business, and each time you stumble or are stung (as in the story above), you carry that experience and make it part of your identity. And slowly but surely, the picture of you starts getting morphed, the picture of you that starts getting built is made up of pieces from an entirely different puzzle. There is no resemblance to the picture on the box, and this means that everything has been forced into place, ready to fall apart with the slightest nudge.

Why is it important to know our core values?

Knowing our core values is crucial. It helps us stay steadfast in the face of adversity as our core; our inner knowing can weather a lot more than our outer being. It helps us to be more decisive because we begin to honor ourselves through each decision we make. Knowing our core values also helps us align better with the external world, in the interactions we have and the relationships we build. It also helps us understand why we feel triggered in some circumstances.

As I embarked on my path to self-discovery, I reconnected with my core self, I recognized my core values of love, freedom, and growth. Soon enough, I was sure of every decision I made. Unfazed by judgment, I realized that every person has different core values and naturally would approach life differently. As long as I approached my life from my core values, I was being true to myself. And that is the only truth that matters!

It also helped me show up with more understanding and compassion. I stopped comparing because I realized each one of us has a different set of core values, and we are all busy operating from our individual blueprint.

So now that you understand the importance of core values, how do you go about discovering them?

When I joined my coaching program, my master coach Ajit asked us to think about our core values. I started by thinking, "I nailed this, I have so many," and my ego started drawing up a long list! But the wise man that he is, he knew all too well that we would all start with our set of preconditioned character traits.

He asked us to stack each value against the other, till we came up with our top 3 values. "These values represent your beliefs", he said. "When you take an action, you always come from this place, you will not compromise on these set of values," he emphasized.

As I set out on the exercise, it was an eye opener for me. I understood myself and I understood my frustrations, I understood why certain things though "good ideas" didn't resonate with me on a deeper level. More importantly, I understood the values I was compromising on in an attempt to gain external validation.

As you start this journey, I would invite you to complete the exercise at the end of this chapter. Look at the list and highlight your values, keep comparing your highlighted values against each other to see what is more important for you and resonates the most with you. Repeat till you have your three core values. These values may evolve over time, but they don't drastically change over a daily or weekly basis.

Now that you know your core values, be mindful when you have to do something, take a pause and ask yourself, "Is the action I am about to take in alignment with my core values?"

This alignment to your core values will help ensure that actions you take from now on are in complete alignment to your desires and not driven by a need for external validation.

Core Values Exercise

Reminder: Take time to be mindful when doing your exercises.

1. Read through the list of values on the next page.
2. Highlight your core values.
3. Compare your highlighted values, see which is more important than the other.
4. Keep comparing them and selecting the most important one till you end up with your top 3 values.
5. Once you have your top 3 values, reflect on them. Do you feel they ring true?
6. Record these values on the space given at the end of the list.

Accountability	Courage	Harmony
Adaptability	Creativity	Health
Altruism	Decisiveness	Honesty
Assertiveness	Dependability	Honor
Awareness	Discipline	Hope
Balance	Drive	Humility
Boldness	Efficiency	Humor
Calm	Empathy	Individuality

Candor	Enthusiasm	Inspiring
Charity	Equality	Intelligence
Common sense	Fairness	Justice
Compassion	Fidelity	Kindness
Confidence	Freedom	Logic
Connection	Fun	Love
Consistency	Generosity	Loyalty
Conviction	Gratitude	Openness
Cooperation	Happiness	Optimism
Passion	Patience	Persistence
Playfulness	Purpose	Realistic
Respect	Responsibility	Security
Self-reliance	Selfless	Service
Tolerance	Transparency	Trustworthy
Understanding	Unity	

My Top 3 Core Values Are

_____

_____

_____

CHAPTER 2

Know That You Are Enough

*He who knows that enough is enough
will always have enough.*
—Lao Tzu

HAVE YOU EVER felt that you are not good enough? Have you compared yourself to someone else and felt that you fall short? Have you ever scrolled through social media and instead of feeling inspired, felt you are not enough?

I know that feeling only too well. I had just had my first baby Uma; I was absolutely enamored by her! And like any mother out there, I wanted to do everything right for her. I wanted to be all she deserved and then some. I remember stepping out with Uma for her playtime at our neighborhood community center. I was always amazed by the well-put and organized moms who showed up; they showed up with freshly pureed concoctions for the babies and beautifully baked little treats for the older kids and the moms.

Often, I would look at them and then look at myself. I saw so many shortcomings. I would recollect the mad dash I had each morning to get my daughter and myself dressed and ready to run out the door. I would remember the chaos that surrounded me and the last-minute running around I seemed to be doing all the time. I saw faults in myself and would get dejected at seeing how much I lacked. I would feel that I could never be the picture of poise and grace that my baby deserved.

It took me a few more years to realize that I am the mother my baby needs. Uma is a spontaneous kid, an old soul, she thrives on social interactions, experiences, and new learnings. She is always full of awe and wonder and keen to learn more and more about the world that surrounds her.

There were reasons why my days looked chaotic in comparison to others.

In those early days, we would make monthly trips from our hometown of Ottawa to Toronto where the rest of our family resided. It was a tough weekend trip with a newborn and often threw our schedules off, but we got to visit our families and have our daughter enjoy and bask in the love and attention of her great grandmother, her grandparents, and her aunts and uncles.

In addition, very often in those early years when Uma was just a little baby, my friends would drop in without much notice; there was no excessive coordination of calendars. Uma was joyful during these interactions. She learned so much from each and every one of my friends. To this day, she has a deep relationship with each of them. And for me, my friends are among my greatest joys, we are now in different cities, but those days when we would have spontaneous visits, chatting and laughing and enjoying each other's company late into the night are among my most cherished memories.

All that connection, the social interactions, the spontaneity were in fact all those ingredients that my little girl's soul needed to thrive and grow into her true expression. I was and am enough for myself and my baby.

And when it comes to poise and grace, I now realize mine comes in the form of my ability to tackle last-minute changes to our plans, in my capacity to make my home a welcoming place for everyone we meet, and in my spontaneity to hit the road and plan weekend trips and excursions at the drop of a hat. We are each blessed with the gifts that meet our soul print, and this is the message we need to understand that we are each of us enough in our own way.

Why is it important to know and feel that you are enough?

When you don't feel that you are enough, you feel sad, dejected. You feel severely lacking in what it takes to be your true self. You begin to build a mindset of measuring yourself against others and when you do so, you are incapable of seeing your gifts. You see faults and fail to recognize your strengths. More importantly, you lose conviction in the decisions you make and your reasons for those decisions. You become inauthentic as you try to mimic the people around you, and you become a follower rather than a leader. You lose your self-worth.

What does it mean to be enough?

To be enough is to know with full conviction that you have all the tools you need to live your life in this moment. It means that you are doing your best at any given time and you do not need to measure yourself with an external yardstick to see proof of this.

If I am enough, does that mean I do not need to grow and evolve?

Being enough does not take away the fact that we need to actively grow and evolve. In fact, it means that you are actively learning, growing and evolving, and you are driven to do so by your soul, by your own desire to be a better version of you today than you were the previous day. It means that your growth and evolution is at your own pace and in the areas that your soul desires, and that this growth is taking place without a sense of urgency or comparison, rather with a sense of authenticity and joy in the journey.

We are each a unique expression of cosmic energy; we each have been given the tools to fulfill our life's purpose and we are each enough.

When you truly believe you are enough, you are deeply connected to your spirit and you begin to follow your soul purpose.

When you know you are enough, it increases your understanding of your self-worth. You are able to meet challenges from a place of resilience and conviction in your strength and your capabilities. You automatically operate from a place of knowing, and as you operate from this deep knowing, you realize that your actions are automatically being validated by you.

When you know you are enough, you experience internal validation.

Awesome Self Exercise:

Take some time to reflect and journal by answering the following questions:

Reflect on your own unique qualities, talents, and strengths.

Write them down and acknowledge them. Recognize that these qualities make you who you are and contribute to your worthiness.

_____

_____

_____

_____

Write in your journal about situations where you have felt inadequate or not good enough. Explore the underlying beliefs and thoughts associated with these feelings. Then, challenge those beliefs by providing evidence of your worth and accomplishments.

_____

_____

_____

_____

Create positive affirmations that reinforce your belief in your own worthiness. For example, "I am enough exactly as I am," or "I embrace my unique qualities and trust in my own path."

_____

_____

_____

_____

Embrace the idea that imperfections are part of being human. Instead of striving for perfection, focus on progress and growth. Celebrate your achievements, no matter how small they may seem.

_____

_____

_____

_____

CHAPTER 3

Self-awareness

All things are created twice, but not all first creations are by conscious design. In our personal lives, if we do not develop our own self-awareness and become responsible for first creations, we empower other people and circumstances outside our Circle of Influence to shape much of our lives by default.
—Stephen Covey

DO YOU EVER feel misunderstood? Do you feel like people don't get you?

How is it possible for someone to get you if you haven't taken the time to know yourself?

Do you really know yourself? Not your habits, not your routines, not your likes or dislikes, but your spirit—do you truly know your spirit?

SELF-AWARENESS

When we were kids, one of the first essays we were asked to write in our school was titled "Myself" and it was meant to be an essay about ourselves.

It was a simple enough essay from the perspective of a 3-year-old. It went something like: "My name is Aarti. I am three years old. I live at home with my mama and papa. I have a pet dog. Her name is coffee toffee. I go to Tiny Tots nursery school. I love my family very much."

What a beautiful and simple essay from the perspective of a kid. As the years progress and the experiences grow, you would imagine the essay would evolve in beauty and complexity. But most of us are stuck in the essay structure of a 3-year-old. Adding relationships and a job title but little else.

As my kids were growing up, I started realizing that as I hung out with other parents, our conversations would always revolve around our kids, our role as parents and our new identities. And while these conversations helped us normalize the madness and craziness and share and exchange tips, I would always leave yearning for more.

Where were we as individuals? Who were we? What are the things that changed within us? What transformed? What were the reasons for those transformations? How were we following our dreams and fulfilling our desires? There was so much to ask and to know and to explore and to figure, and yet we were all stuck in the merest descriptions of ourselves: the essay of a 3-year-old.

I feel a lot of the conversations don't go deep as we do not take the time to connect with ourselves. Connecting with ourselves takes time, patience and practice in a world where we have been conditioned to always be reactive to the outside world.

Why is it important for you to get to know yourself?

Think about those pivotal moments in stories, movies, or real life where trust defines the turning point—someone says, "I knew I could trust them because I know who they are." Now imagine what it would mean to be able to say that to yourself. To know yourself so deeply that in moments of adversity, you trust your decisions and character without hesitation. This is the power of self-awareness: cultivating the unshakable belief that no matter the circumstances, you know who you are and what you stand for.

When you get to know yourself deeper, connect with yourself deeper, that is exactly the unflappable conviction you will experience on a daily basis! In good times and in bad, in moments of adversity or a new challenge, you will experience self-worth and self-trust as never before.

Because in that knowing, in that constant reconnection with yourself lies the capacity to define the terms on which you want to live, to draw the path that you want to take and to define the future you want. With that knowing also comes alignment. Alignment to your strengths, to your visions, to your goals. Once you achieve this alignment, it gets easy to resist peer pressure, societal expectations, and cultural norms. It is easy to be who you are meant to be and to evolve to who you want to be. It is easy to validate yourself for your actions

SELF-AWARENESS

How well do you know yourself?

Can you truly sit down and define who you are without the crutches of your roles and responsibilities? Do not get me wrong, you must honor the roles you play and know you are privileged to be a child, a sibling, a partner, a parent, a friend. And alongside that, you also need to acknowledge your spirit that is far more vast and expansive to be contained within the descriptions of your roles.

To know yourself deeply, to reconnect with yourself, to be self-aware, you will need to start by loving yourself truly, sincerely, and deeply. Love your scars, love your flaws, love yourself enough that you take out time to be with you, without any distractions or demands. As you begin to love yourself, you will experience a deep self-awareness, one that will enable you to let go of the habits, the thoughts, the limiting beliefs that no longer serve you and you will continue to evolve. And most important of all, you will be able to do this without hurt, judgment, or criticism.

As I coach my clients, the question that stumps them the most is what do you love about yourself?

After thinking for several minutes, they might come up with

- I <insert task> very well for <insert person / corporation name>

- I take care of _<insert person/relationship/pet>___

- I am a good _<insert role>___

As I embarked on my journey, I too spent the most time thinking about this: What do I love about myself?

I was sitting home alone one day, and as I was trying to figure out what I love about myself, I started listing things, but as I looked at the list, I realized they were things that others loved about me. I was dissatisfied! I turned to my husband and kids that evening and asked them what they loved about me. Despite the things they listed, I was dissatisfied.

You see, I had the longest relationship with myself and I was incapable of listing what I loved about myself, and therefore, nothing rang true. I listed things like:

My sense of humor

My ability to move to different cities and adapt

My ability to have deep conversations

But I was craving depth and I didn't find that depth in my answers, I felt these were versions of stories that someone else had shared with me. I wanted my own answers; my soul was yearning for me to connect with it and get to know it!

This led to a long journey of understanding myself from the place of my experiences, my triggers, my fears, my insecurities, my moral values, my strengths and my joys.

SELF-AWARENESS

Today, my list is way more complex. Here are a few things that showed up on my list:

- I love that I want to live life to the fullest - from every rock bottom, I have bounced back much faster than even I had imagined. My scars remind me of the lessons and the wisdom I have gained but have not changed my identity.

- I love my imagination - it is limitless, and through my imagination I have managed to do so many different things in life. I have always been able to figure out a way to make things happen.

- I love my positivity - through some of the worst times, I was able to see at least one silver lining and hang onto it till the sun came out.

- I love my ability to feel compassion - I can feel my heart expand so much as it brings the entire earth and all living things into its embrace.

I would now urge you to reconnect with yourself and to do this from a place of love where you identify the things that you truly love about yourself.

Remember, when you operate from a place of love and self-awareness, you experience a deep level of self-validation.

You further build your internal validation muscle!

True Self Exercise:

Set aside some time to journal about your true self. Reflect on your experiences, triggers, fears, insecurities, values, strengths, and joys. Write freely and without judgment, allowing your thoughts and emotions to flow onto the pages.

_____

_____

_____

_____

_____

_____

_____

_____

_____

_____

_____

_____

SELF-AWARENESS

Create a list of things you genuinely love about yourself. Dig deep and go beyond surface-level characteristics. Focus on your personal growth, resilience, unique qualities, and inner strengths. Write down as many things as you can, embracing both the small and significant aspects of who you are.

_____

_____

_____

_____

Recall moments from your childhood when you felt the most authentic and connected to yourself. What activities brought you joy? What qualities did you possess that made you feel alive? Reflect on those memories and consider how you can reintegrate elements of your childhood self into your present life.

_____

_____

_____

_____

Identify an aspect of yourself that you have been suppressing or hiding. It could be a talent, a passion, or a personal belief. Take a step toward expressing that aspect authentically. This could involve sharing it with a trusted friend, finding a creative outlet for it, or simply embracing it more fully in your daily life.

_____

_____

_____

_____

Remember, these exercises are meant to support your journey of self-awareness and self-discovery. Take your time, be patient with yourself, and embrace the process of getting to know and love the true essence of who you are.

Section 2

RECLAIM YOUR SPACE

Now that you have reconnected with your inner self and opened up to the wonder, the unique magic that is you, you should feel stronger, more confident, and empowered in your knowingness and in the awareness of your true spirit.

In the following section, you will be reclaiming yourself by freeing yourself from the thoughts, the beliefs, the patterns that have been limiting you and holding you back. As you break free from the chains of your past, you will be able to soar, higher and farther than your wildest dreams.

CHAPTER 4

Adjust Your Hindsight Window

*I have no desire to suffer twice,
in reality and then in retrospect.*
—Sophocles, Oedipus Rex

HAVE YOU TRULY resolved your failures or disappointments from the past? Do you recollect old stories with a sense of regret, or are you able to recall them from a place of learning? Do you constantly chide yourself for mistakes or missed opportunities?

If self-doubt creeps in when you look back at your past (your hindsight window) and you only remember selective information, your memories are not fully true, so I call it a foggy hindsight window.

As I was working with a client, I noticed how she constantly doubted herself. She kept referring to herself as incapable; therefore, no matter what decision she made, she always believed had she made a different decision the outcome would have been "better."

As I was talking to her, I noticed that she constantly criticized herself for the decisions she had made in the past. During one of our sessions, I stopped her mid-story and urged her to set herself back in time and see her decisions through the lens of her younger version.

As she recounted the same story again, I asked her these questions: How old were you at the time? Has that younger version of you ever had a similar experience before then? How experienced were you in that area at that time? Who was in your support circle? How old were they? Did they have the experience necessary to support you better? Can you think of the challenges perhaps they were facing in their personal life? What resources did they have at that time? What resources did you have at the time?

And as she started recounting the story with these factual details, she broke down in tears. She realized how harsh she had been to herself and the many years she had held onto thoughts and stories that were holding her back. Most importantly, she was ready to shed her old identity and try on a new, more empowered one.

I remember when I first looked back into my hindsight window. You see, I always considered myself mediocre. When I got a job, I would attribute it to luck, when I got recognition, I would attribute it to the kindness of the person who recognized me. Despite a successful IT career, I considered myself unsmart and incapable of anything intellectual.

As I was working on myself, I decided to look into my hindsight window and to go back in time to where I picked this belief.

It came back to me very clearly. I was to start Grade 10 in a school in Oman where our family had recently relocated. I had given an entrance exam to be accepted into the school. I remember holding the questionnaire in my hand and feeling stunned, shocked, and overwhelmed. The questions made no sense to me. I drew a blank. The school called and told my parents they wouldn't accept me in Grade 10. I was ashamed and guilty; I begged for a second chance. I managed to do better and got accepted in Grade 10, but I did miserably thereon and each exam after that. I was terrified that I would fail. I considered myself lucky when I passed, and in some subjects I did so by the skin of my teeth.

I tried my own suggestion to step back in time, recreate those circumstances and understand my truth, and I realized there was a different way to recount this story.

I was a well-rounded student in my school in Mumbai. I was above average, participated in sports, was on the student council. I was a little weak in elective languages and needed help in math, but overall, I managed well. When I went to give that entrance exam, I was pretty confident of myself. I had no idea that the school followed a completely different curriculum. I was stumped when I saw that questionnaire. I had not covered most of the topics in my previous school. When I begged for a second chance and got through, it wasn't because I had miraculously caught up to the curriculum; rather, it was because I had desperately crammed the material to pass the entrance exam. And from that time on, with a lack of foundational knowledge, I performed poorly in my exams. I remembered a teacher using the word "mediocre" to describe me. It was an easy explanation for my poor performance, and I made it a part of my identity, one that I would believe for another 20 odd years.

Once I could recount my story with the factual information, I was able to shed the unsmart and mediocre identity I had adopted. I now know that my poor performance was a result of my circumstances and the decisions I made as a 15-year-old.

Having this knowledge has given me the confidence to be an entrepreneur and to learn many new skills such as marketing, sales, business planning, etc. Today, when I lack knowledge, I have a can-do attitude because I know that each one of us is capable given the right tools and time.

Why does your hindsight window matter?

You may have gone through some tough experiences in your life; the objective of these experiences was to give you the opportunity to learn and grow. However, there may have been instances when the experience was so big that you got attached to it and that you made the experience part of your identity.

As opposed to emerging with the learning, you emerged with the baggage—the event, the characters, the hardships. When you do this, you enable a victim mindset, where you feel that life is happening to you and you have no control over the outcomes and when you take on the victim mindset. You rob yourself of the opportunity to celebrate your hero's journey, the journey that highlights how you came out the other end of a challenge or tough situation. Without your hero's journey, you end up doubting yourself, you lose self-confidence and become unsure of your abilities. Worst of all, you end up taking on an identity that disempowers you.

How do I clean my foggy hindsight window?

Look at your life, look at your ups and your downs, look at your life events through the lens of your age, experience, and knowledge at that point in time. Recollect the resources you had access to, recreate the scenario and acknowledge your actions within the constraints.

As you go through these steps, try and distill the growth you experienced. If at any point of those experiences you remember being judged, bring back that judgment and assess it. Ask yourself if, as a kind, empathetic, and compassionate human, would you pass the same remarks or criticisms to someone within your circumstance? The intent here is not to make excuses for yourself. Rather, it is to understand yourself and to ensure that you have grown and evolved to be more experienced and confident than you were and to experience this growth without taking on any negative identities.

ADJUST YOUR HINDSIGHT WINDOW

If you feel you haven't learned, are you willing to put in the effort to learn? Remember, through every action we take, we either learn and proceed or we learn and re-try.

Does your self-doubt stem from a foggy hindsight window? Do you need to clean it?

It is important for you to take the time to revisit and adjust your hindsight window.

Know that when you look back to a point in time, you are already more aware and experienced than you were then. You have already seen the outcome, so it is easy to think of the alternate path. When you keep berating yourself for the decisions you made, you lose your trust in yourself.

A lack of self-trust will most definitely lead to self-doubt, which shows up as indecisiveness when you need to make a decision, which in turn leads to worry and anxiety when you finally do take an action.

As you begin to look into your hindsight window with a discerning and fair eye, you will be able to be more confident. You will feel more empowered as you will see yourself not as a victim but rather as a doer and learner.

You will begin to take confident action and you will take another step toward a deeper sense of inner validation.

Hindsight Window Exercise

Take some time to think about significant events or decisions from your past that you often recall with regret or self-criticism. Write them down and identify the emotions associated with them.

_____

_____

_____

_____

_____

For each event or decision, step back in time and try to recreate the circumstances as accurately as possible. Consider your age, experience, knowledge and the resources available to you at that time. Write down these details for each situation.

_____

_____

_____

_____

_____

ADJUST YOUR HINDSIGHT WINDOW

With the factual information in hand, reassess your actions in light of the circumstances. Recognize the limitations or challenges you faced and how they influenced your choices. Avoid harsh self-judgment and aim for a fair evaluation.

_____

_____

_____

_____

Look for moments of growth and learning within each experience. Ask yourself what lessons you gained from those situations and how they have contributed to your personal development. Write down the insights and realizations you've gained.

_____

_____

_____

_____

If you recall being judged by others during those events, bring back those judgments and assess them objectively. Ask yourself if, as a kind and compassionate person, you would pass the same judgments on someone else in a similar situation. Challenge any unfair criticisms and reframe them with empathy and understanding.

_____

_____

_____

_____

Commit to ongoing learning: If you identify areas where you feel you haven't learned or grown as much as you'd like, make a commitment to invest in your personal development. Determine specific steps you can take to acquire the knowledge or skills needed to overcome those limitations.

_____

_____

_____

_____

Remember, these exercises are meant to be introspective and empowering. Take your time with each step and be gentle with yourself throughout the process. By adjusting your hindsight window, you can cultivate a more compassionate and empowering perspective on your past experiences, which will ultimately help you overcome self-doubt.

CHAPTER 5

Be Your Own Cheerleader

*Oh I think that I found myself a cheerleader,
She is always right there when I need her.*
Lyrics: Cheerleader by Omi

ARE YOU CHEERED on, encouraged, and motivated throughout your day? Do you have a troupe of cheerleaders encouraging you ahead, or do you experience judgment that continuously brings you down?

What about your self-talk, is it motivating, empowering, and cheering you on, or is it holding harsh judgments toward you?

We all have an inner voice. It could be either our cheerleader or an unforgiving judge, and if our inner voice is a judge, it could be one of the worst tenants we could have in our brain. It often holds us back from our fullest potential to experience joy, happiness, bliss, love, and growth.

BE YOUR OWN CHEERLEADER

It was a special week. My husband's 40th birthday was coming up. He had returned from a seven-month work tour in South Sudan, making this birthday extra special for all of us as a family. To make this occasion even more "momentous," we had just been posted to a new town and had moved into our new home.

The truck with our contents arrived on a Tuesday and the unpackers on Wednesday. While my husband was running errands and coordinating the various contractors and arranging appointments to make sure the house was fixed, I was juggling setting up the house with my two daughters (then 8 and 5) in tow.

I had a day to get us and our new home organized so we could host our families (13 people) for a long weekend of celebrations. I squeezed every minute I could from the 30 odd hours I had to get us in a fully functional home.

By the time the first of our guests arrived, I had done it!

The house was set up, most of the boxes unpacked, everyone's rooms were ready. I even managed to cook a few meals and prep for a BBQ; I was ready! As everyone started trickling in and the celebrations started, I found myself being apologetic for every little thing: "I am sorry, I haven't had a chance to unpack the fancy dishes," " I am sorry the dinner is quite simple," " I am sorry, I didn't get a chance to stock up the pantry," and on and on. I looked at every face around me hoping to get praise for the impossible feat that I had managed.

COACH AARTI

When I heard the praise from my parents, I wondered if it was biased since no one else echoed it. When I heard the praise from my brother, I was convinced that he was being kind as he has always been my biggest supporter. When my husband praised me, I was sure he did so out of the unconditional love he showers me with.

I kept looking at the ones who held back the praise and tried to look at myself through their eyes to see the flaws or shortcomings that they "obviously" saw in me. And so I spent the weekend constantly judging myself.

As I look back today, I realize that if anyone else had pulled off what I had, I would be in absolute awe of them. I would have been amazed with the planning, the effort, and the love they had put into making me welcome in their home. And yet that weekend and for years after that weekend, I was incapable of seeing myself for the strengths I possess. I had an inner critic much harsher than any critic I would encounter.

It was only a few years ago that I realized something phenomenal—I realized that I am the one who needs to cheer me on!

As I became my own cheerleader, when others cheered me on, I believed them and considered them part of my cheerleading squad. I learned to celebrate with them and share more moments with them, and for those who didn't, well, I let them have their opinions without it altering my ability to recognize myself, celebrate my achievements, and cheer myself on to do more and better. I let them slip away so that I could surround myself with even more cheerleaders!

Today, I have evolved. When I do anything, even an act I do for others, I do it because my heart desires it. I do as much as I can without compromising on my values, and I take the time to recognize my efforts. I no longer spend precious time wondering what someone might think of me or being concerned about what someone might say about me. This is because today, my biggest cheerleader goes everywhere with me!

Why is it important to cheer ourselves on?

When you don't cheer yourself on and when you house a harsh inner critic, you do not stand up for yourself. You constantly seek out external clues to tell you how you are doing. You consistently try to read into how others look at you, what they might be thinking about you and you fall into the trap of being a people-pleaser. Everything that you do is driven by a desire to please others, you start drifting away from your own priorities and you stop recognizing and enjoying your achievements. Instead, you are focused on the absence of validation from those present. You lose your ability to be present with yourself and for yourself. You stop recognizing your gifts, your talents, your superpowers!

Does being your own cheerleader make you self-absorbed?

Not at all, when you are a cheerleader, you bring those skills to everyone in your life. It becomes second nature to cheer. Your inner judge who passes judgment not only on you but on others as well gets subdued, and this is one of the most selfless ways to celebrate and encourage yourself and those around you.

How do we build our cheerleading muscles?

Observe your inner judge. As it gets ready to say something unkind (directed toward yourself or someone else), catch that thought and analyze it. Discern the thought, dismiss anything that is disempowering and choose the one that empowers you.

How do we catch our thoughts?

Catching thoughts is one of the toughest things to do. We are used to thinking a mile a minute, moving from one thought to another. When you catch a thought and analyze it, you give yourself the power to pause, get self-aware, and discern. As a thought occurs to you and you pause, get curious about that thought, ask yourself, "Why did this thought come up to me?"

As you catch that thought, write it down on a piece of paper.

Reflect on the factual information surrounding the thought. Write down this factual information on a piece of paper.

The factual information is that which cannot be refuted. Such as the place where the incident occurred. The time of day. The people who were present/absent, etc. It is that information that every person in this world will agree with, irrespective of their age, background or association with you.

Now that you have this factual information, assess the thought once again. Is this thought true or false, kind or unkind?

If this thought or judgment is false or unkind, what is the true, kind thought that you would like to replace it with? Write down this thought.

If this thought or judgment is true and it is something that hurts you, ask yourself why it hurts you. Does it hurt because it isn't aligned with your values? If yes, what can you do to start acting in better alignment with your values? Write it down and see this as an opportunity for growth and improvement.

If it hurts but is not in alignment with your values, write down why it is not aligned with your values and your identity and as you write that down.

Now replace your initial thought with a more empowered one.

My core values are _____. I do not care about any judgment about _____ as it does not align with my core values.

Or

My core values are _____. I just learned I could better align with my values by improving how I do_____. I will take ___ steps to grow from here.

Be the change you want to see. If you wish that people were kinder, well start by being kind to yourself first and then to everyone else around you. When it comes to harsh judgments, let the buck stop at you.

Cheer yourself on and start enjoying your internal validation

Catch Your Thoughts Exercise

Take a few moments to observe and catch negative or judgmental thoughts that arise in your mind. Write them down on a piece of paper. By bringing awareness to these thoughts, you can start to understand the patterns and triggers behind them.

_____

_____

_____

_____

For each negative thought you've written down, analyze the factual information surrounding it. Write down the objective details related to the thought, such as the time, place and people involved. This exercise helps separate factual information from subjective judgments.

_____

_____

_____

_____

_____

Once you've identified a negative thought, challenge its truthfulness and kindness. If the thought is false or unkind, replace it with a more empowering and compassionate thought. Write down the new thought and repeat it to yourself whenever the negative thought arises.

_____

_____

_____

_____

_____

Reflect on your core values and identify how the negative thoughts or judgments might conflict with them. If a judgment hurts because it isn't aligned with your values, consider what steps you can take to better align your actions with those values. Write down specific actions you can take to grow and improve in those areas.

_____

_____

_____

_____

_____

Take time to recognize and celebrate your achievements, no matter how small they may seem. Make a list of accomplishments or positive qualities you possess and revisit it regularly to remind yourself of your strengths. Practice self-compassion and acknowledge your efforts and progress.

_____

_____

_____

_____

Extend your cheerleading skills beyond yourself. Practice kindness and support toward others in your life. Offer genuine praise and encouragement to those around you, and be a positive force in their lives.

Remember, being a cheerleader for others doesn't diminish your ability to cheer for yourself. Identify below some of the ways in which you will start cheering others around you.

_____

_____

_____

_____

CHAPTER 6

Compassion and Forgiveness

In compassion and grace, be like the sun...
In concealing other's faults, be like the night...
In generosity and helping others, be like a river...
In anger and fury, be like dead...
In modesty and humility, be like the earth...
In tolerance, be like the sea...
Either appear as you are, or be as you appear...
—Rumi

HAVE YOU EVER felt wronged? Do you feel anger, resentment and revenge take over your mental peace when you think of certain people or incidents?

When was the last time you felt an overflow of compassion—compassion so vast that it drew a warm and loving bubble around you? When was the last time you truly forgave yourself with grace, wholeheartedness, compassion and kindness?

COMPASSION AND FORGIVENESS

Compassion in its truest form makes one feel safe, loved and understood. It is an energy that if you are fully enveloped in it, it will overflow and touch everyone around it. It does not discriminate and it cannot hold negative energy, and therefore to truly be compassionate toward yourself, you must practice forgiveness, and to truly forgive, you need to be compassionate. However, there is an important realization you need here that forgiveness and compassion do not discriminate. Therefore, if you want to forgive yourself and be compassionate toward yourself, you will have to extend it beyond yourself.

During one of my growth quests, I did a timeline. The timeline listed out all the ups and downs in my life on a chart. As I looked through it, I had a lump in my throat. I had been through quite a bit; however, always one to soldier on, I had never really taken pause to reflect what each event meant in terms of fear, anger, shock, hurt and a multitude of different emotions directed toward myself and those external to me.

As I did this timeline, I started to take the time to acknowledge the impact that past events, including the actions of others, had on my life. I was able to acknowledge the impact of the experiences; however, I was not able to let go.

The events and incidents that had all been pulled up from under the rug now seemed to be floating all around me, and I felt like I was reliving them constantly. I was no longer able to stay present. I didn't understand—the lessons had been distilled and the file was no longer needed. Yet it kept surfacing, till I realized the next step that I needed to take: I needed to forgive.

To truly reclaim your space, you need to empty your heart of all the hurt, the anger and the drama it is holding onto. This step is not an easy one, but with compassion, you can get there.

I went through a period when I was misunderstood, and a lot of hurtful things were said about me and my loved ones. I knew that my conscience was clear, but I spent weeks and months hurting over the words that were said. I could never imagine getting past that hurt. That is when I realized, I was angry and unforgiving not only to the people who hurt me but also toward my younger self that let them hurt me.

We are largely compassionate beings, but to take compassion to the next level, to truly be enveloped in the loving comfort of compassion, you will have to extend it beyond yourself, including those who you feel have wronged you. This is where I was stuck. How could I be compassionate without being forgiving and if I was incapable of forgiving, how could I expand and be free? For till we truly forgive and let go, we are never really free.

Forgiveness and compassion became really important to me as I wanted to reclaim the space that past stories, hurt and pain were taking up in my beingness. I wanted to experience complete freedom to be me—my authentic self!

COMPASSION AND FORGIVENESS

Why is forgiving so hard?

In the past, whenever I would think of forgiveness, it always seemed hard!

In my world, it meant letting someone get away! I was ready for my six-phase meditation certification call with Vishen Lakhiani, the creator of the six-phase meditation. It is one of the most known meditation tracks, and I have been practicing it for years now. If you are familiar with the six phases, you will realize that compassion and forgiveness are two of the six phases of this powerful technique. As Vishen explained this meditation tool to us and we raised questions, he understood the hesitancy in letting go.

He very eloquently clarified that forgiveness does not mean you take away the charge or you stop holding the perpetrator accountable for their wrong doing. It simply means that you no longer hold a negative charge or a negative emotion in your heart. You have the grace to see the earlier version of yourself or the other person (as the case may be) as a fellow human, and you can forgive them on a spiritual level. From here, you can let go with grace for smaller offenses or continue to hold someone accountable for bigger indiscretions.

From this understanding, I was suddenly able to forgive, and I realized how much better I felt. I was no longer the vessel for revenge, anger or hurt. As I started practicing this forgiveness, I was amazed. Every act of forgiveness made me feel lighter and lighter. I was able to move past the pain and anger that I thought I would carry forever. Today

I hold myself sacred and would not let a similar incident repeat. I learned the lesson that the universe wanted me to learn and I have let go.

When you forgive, you let go of the hold the past has on you; the negative energy that you are holding just dissipates. You also experience humility, for to forgive also entails quieting your ego that desperately wants to protect you by hanging on to every negative experience. As you forgive, there are two more powerful skills you build: discernment and surrender.

You learn to discern the event, removing the drama that surrounds it and sticking to the facts. You learn to be fair, and through this fairness, you are able to learn the lesson that you were meant to learn. The actions that follow are fair and reasonable, and then you learn to surrender to the powers that be to enforce the consequences that are not yours to enforce. And finally, you increase your resonance as a deeply compassionate being, for every act of forgiveness is a testament to how deeply you honor yourself.

How do you forgive?

Forgiveness is one of the toughest exercises you will complete in this book as your ego will not want you to let go.

Therefore, to forgive, I will start you off by helping you understand what it means to not forgive. For this demonstration and understanding, I will have you focus on someone external to you.

COMPASSION AND FORGIVENESS

Bring to mind an incident or an event that upset you. I would recommend starting with something small. As you exercise and grow your compassion and forgiveness muscles, you can move to bigger incidents.

Bring to mind the person(s) that you hold responsible. Think of them. Continue to think of them and notice how you feel. Is your jaw clenched? Are your fists clenched? Is your breathing shallow? Does your chest feel tight? What about your thoughts? Are they disempowered thoughts? Are they negative and vicious?

Now, assign a toxicity to everything you are feeling inside. Imagine a toxic chemical seeping into your body; the more vengeance, negativity and viciousness you feel, the more this toxic soup increases in your body. Now see how this toxicity is harming you, damaging your cells, your nerves and your being. See it slowly eating away at your health from the inside and see it holding you back from leading your life on your terms. See it holding you back from showing up for yourself and for the ones that truly matter to you.

Do you see the impact of being unforgiving?

The only person coming to harm is you, so to forgive another is also an act of love directed to yourself.

Now, take a deep breath and see this incident from the lens of curiosity. What were the circumstances around which the incident happened? How could you account for someone's wrongdoing? Could it be ignorance, lack of understanding, circumstances out of their control? Can you, from this place, show them empathy, say the words, "I forgive you"? As you repeat the words "I forgive you," see the toxicity in your body leave you, see how you feel. Can you breathe better? Do you feel lighter?

So how do I continue to practice forgiveness?

Begin to see yourself as a compassionate being. Tell yourself that you will try to understand the situation no matter how difficult. Each time you are reminded of an event or person that hurt you, bring it to the forefront. Can you picture the person that hurt you once again? It could be a past version of you or someone external to you. Observe this person from a place of compassion. Get curious: What is their life like (at the point of time when the event occurred) both from a material and a spiritual view point?

What are some of the challenges that they might have faced in their past or that they are currently facing? What could have shaped them to be the way they are? What could have caused them to act in the way they did? What was their childhood like?

Remember if it is someone external to you and if you don't know them well, you can imagine what could have made them act the way they did. Maybe they lacked guidance, love, empathy, maybe they didn't know better, maybe they were trying to protect someone or something, maybe they were acting from a place of fear or scarcity. As you try to see them from this lens, you realize they are human, capable of making errors just like you. You can

COMPASSION AND FORGIVENESS

take away the godlike persona you had given them to be perfect and flawless.

From this place of understanding, can you reflect that the incident occurred for you to learn something of value? Those hurtful incidents and people play the role of a catalyst that will push you to your growth edge.

And finally, from this place of knowing, you will need to let go, to release the hold the past has on you and say, "I forgive you. I learned what I needed to from my experience with you and I forgive you. May you too have the good fortune to learn from that experience."

Continue this practice of compassion and forgiveness toward everyone you hold a negative charge against, including yourself. Most of us need to forgive our younger selves for the mistakes that we have made.

Exercising compassion and forgiveness toward others and yourself will have a big impact on your ability to stand up and take your space unapologetically. Compassion grows exponentially. As you express compassion to yourself, you realize you have the space and energy to show compassion to others around you, and as you get more compassionate, you are able to forgive more quickly and fully. This leads to a beautiful space of joy, happiness, ease, grace and expansiveness in your life. You experience that sanctity of your space and freedom to fully be yourself.

As you begin to exercise compassion and forgiveness, you gain freedom from your ego and your past, which in turn will bring you closer to the internal validation that you seek.

Forgiveness Exercise

Reflect on a recent incident: Think of a small incident that upset you recently. Write down your feelings, thoughts, and the negative charge associated with it.

_____

_____

_____

_____

_____

Practice compassion by trying to understand the situation from the other person's perspective. Write down their possible challenges or circumstances that might have influenced their actions.

_____

_____

_____

_____

_____

COMPASSION AND FORGIVENESS

Release the hold this incident has on you by consciously forgiving and letting go. Write a forgiveness statement expressing your understanding and willingness to release the negative emotions associated with the incident.

_____

_____

_____

_____

_____

Start a forgiveness journal to track your progress in cultivating forgiveness and compassion. Write about situations, people, or incidents that you are working on forgiving. Reflect on your growing understanding and empathy toward these situations and individuals. Notice the positive changes in your own well-being and relationships as you continue to practice forgiveness.

_____

_____

_____

_____

_____

Engage in acts of compassion and kindness toward yourself and others. Look for opportunities to offer forgiveness, understanding, and support to people around you. It could be a kind gesture, a listening ear, or a sincere apology. Each act of kindness and forgiveness strengthens your compassionate nature and contributes to a more expansive and free space for you to operate from.

_____

_____

_____

_____

Remember, forgiveness is a personal journey, and these exercises are meant to support your process of cultivating compassion and forgiveness first for yourself and then extend it to those who have a hold on you. Adjust them as needed to suit your preferences and circumstances.

CHAPTER 7

Redesign Your Reality

*Your imagination and your reality are always
in a beautiful dance, weaving and responding to
each other. Your imagination creates your reality,
and your reality fuels your imagination.*
—Aarti Mehta-Nayyar

AS YOU GO about your days, do you have a sense that you are not feeling supported? Do you feel that your physical environment is holding you back from being the better version of yourself that you would like to be?

Our reality is a result of our perception of the world based on our past experiences. Therefore, our past experiences will continue to dictate our future, that is, until we intervene. While we are unable to change the past, we can totally break the cycle and influence our movement into the future by redesigning our present state—by intentionally and mindfully designing the current moment—which will gradually slip into the past and help us toward a more intentional future.

There are three dimensions to our reality:

- Mindset: addressed in the first section
- Physical environment: addressed in this chapter
- Social context: addressed in the third section

Very often, we overlook the impact our physical environment has on our emotions and frame of mind.

I was working with a client who was working toward a healthier version of himself. We had had a couple of sessions, and he had gained clarity of his health goals and had started following a routine. However, he was skeptical about his success. "I don't know Aarti, every day I keep up with my commitment; I do the tasks I am meant to, but I feel any moment I will slip and stumble. I feel like an imposter; I feel like I will be right where I started."

As we talked and I asked questions, what we unraveled was fascinating. My client's environment was not enabling him to live his vision. He told me his routine involved arriving home famished and hungry and then trying to figure out something healthy to eat for dinner. He struggled to not reach for the beer sitting chilled in the fridge or the chips in his cupboard. He missed his morning alarm most days because he passed out watching TV.

No wonder he felt lost; his external reality did not match up with his internal visions and desires. It didn't keep up with the person he was evolving into.

We talked about improving his environment such that it supported his new version. Here are some of the things he changed:

- He shopped for dinner on the weekend and prepared food a couple of times a week. He always froze one portion for an "emergency."

- He moved his beer out of the fridge, so it was no longer chilled and tempting him.

- He made little bags of healthy seeds and nuts that he carried in his pocket and kept on his countertop.

- He cleaned his fridge and cupboards of junk food.

- He put an alarm to remind him to turn off his TV and go to bed at a set time each night.

He checked in with me after making the changes we discussed and he was ecstatic. He mentioned how he loves opening the fridge and seeing these beautifully pre-prepared salads and meals waiting for him. He feels a sense of pride just opening his fridge. He feels very driven when he sees the healthy snacking options he has around him, and when he turns off the TV to the reminder of his alarm, he sees himself as a new and empowered person.

Working with him reminded me of the time when I was well on my path of healing. I knew myself better; I reconnected with myself. Yet there was a feeling of frustration, I felt this version of me was in constant struggle to do the things that I desired. It felt it was a challenge to be who I wanted to be. I felt an inner conflict; I felt that I could not achieve my goals as no one supported me and I had to "fight" to be myself.

I remember this one day when I got very upset with my family. I complained that I didn't get time to do the things that mattered to me. My husband was surprised by my outburst as this was the first he was hearing of it. He suggested that on the following Saturday, he would plan an outing with the kids to give me the time I needed. He would keep them busy the entire day. That sounded awesome. I would have an entire day, all the time I needed. As that Saturday rolled around and I said bye to my family, I sat down, my thoughts raced a mile a minute. I had time. What should I do? And suddenly, I was scatterbrained. I couldn't focus on any one thing, and by the time my family came back, I had a dozen unfinished things and a sense of overwhelm and a feeling of guilt and remorse at having missed out on precious family time. I realized I had taken action from an emotional place rather than one of intention.

That is when I realized there was a gap. I was holding my transformations inside me—to be exercised in isolation—it was much like someone would hold a secret. My environment was not aligned to my recently uncovered values, my new beliefs and my new purpose. I knew I needed to do some work so that my environment supported me in the most complete way possible.

I had to redesign my days, giving me time for self-reflection, for self-growth. For being seen by me.

I decided to make a list of things that I needed. Here are some of the things that showed up on my list:

- Uninterrupted time with my family
- Daily meditation practice
- Daily focus on my physical health
- Opportunity to consistently grow and evolve
- A consistent reading habit
- Time to be with my husband
- Time to be with my daughters

Once I had this list, I realized why that one day of "break" was not the solution. I realized my frustrations on my family were misplaced and that I needed to own my transformations and the steps that were required to keep at it.

I realized I needed to redesign my reality.

As I started to set aside time to invest in activities that reflected my interests and purpose in life, as I started to take time to care for myself, to take the time to repeat a mantra to myself or to breathe or enjoy some exercise, my reality changed. As I made myself a priority, others understood my needs and respected that priority as well. They gained clarity in understanding what I needed to feel supported.

What does it mean to redesign your reality and why is it important?

By now you should be better attuned to yourself, your values, your likes, your dislikes and your self-worth and being.

As you deliberately shape your environment in a way that resonates with your core values, aspirations, and self-worth, you will realize that this process holds immense importance. Through this process, you not only validate your internal world but you begin to reinforce its place in the outer world.

By consciously redesigning your reality, you create a nurturing and validating space that supports your goals, visions, and desires. It is a powerful affirmation of your commitment to yourself as you prioritize activities that hold genuine significance to your well-being. In doing so, you send a clear and resounding message to your inner self that you are deserving of your own time, attention, and investment.

As you embark on this transformative journey, you begin to witness a remarkable shift. Your external environment starts to mirror your inner transformation. And your inner transformation gets further fueled by the external support. Those around you start to recognize the changes within you—the growth, the aspirations, and the courage to follow your authentic path. Your cheerleaders become more understanding, supportive, and able to accommodate the changes you require to flourish. You will witness how your internal validation is fueling your external world.

Redesigning your reality also liberates you from the limitations and barriers that may have hindered your progress in the past. It empowers you to intentionally craft an environment that fosters growth, self-expression, and authenticity. By aligning your surroundings with your evolving values, you eliminate unnecessary distractions, triggers, and obstacles that may have held you back. This deliberate act of self-validation allows you to reclaim your power and take charge of your experiences, paving the way for a future that is in harmonious alignment with your truest self.

Through this process of redesign, you honor yourself, acknowledge your worth, and create a supportive ecosystem that fuels your personal growth. It is through this intentional transformation that you unlock your fullest potential and live a life that resonates with your authentic being.

The benefits of redesigning your reality are profound and life-changing. It is an essential step on your path to internal validation.

How would you redesign your day and make yourself a priority? For in making yourself a priority would be the biggest act of approving yourself.

Redesign Your Reality Exercise

Take some time to identify what matters most to you. Consider your values, interests, and aspirations. Make a list of activities and elements that align with your authentic self and contribute to your overall well-being.

_____

_____

_____

_____

_____

Evaluate your physical surroundings, such as your home, workspace, and daily routines. Determine if they are conducive to supporting your goals and reflecting your values. Identify any aspects that may be hindering your progress or causing unnecessary distractions.

_____

_____

_____

_____

_____

Make intentional changes: Once you have identified areas for improvement, start making intentional changes.

_____

_____

_____

_____

Remember, making yourself a priority and redesigning your reality is an act of self-approval and self-validation. By consciously creating an environment that supports your growth and well-being, you empower yourself to live authentically and unlock your fullest potential as you align with your truest self.

Section 3

BUILD YOUR SPIRITUAL ARMOR

It has been quite a journey so far, you have reconnected with your soul, you have uncovered your true spirit, you have cleansed your internal space from any misgivings and have carefully curated the environment around you to best support yourself as you live to realize your fullest expression. The next section is going to help you take that final step—the one where you step out as your true self—unapologetically, where you continue to honor yourself in every situation you encounter. This is going to be a liberating section!

CHAPTER 8

Set Boundaries

Boundaries define us. They define what is me and what is not me. A boundary shows me where I end and someone else begins, leading me to a sense of ownership. Knowing what I am to own and take responsibility for gives me freedom.
—Henry Cloud

YOU KNOW THAT feeling of always being taken for granted; it is such a draining energy. When no one acknowledges your needs. When everyone's needs come way before your own. Do you feel you have to keep changing the dates on your own plans, the timelines on your dreams because something else always comes up? If this rings true, it is time for you to think about boundaries.

I recently had a heartfelt conversation with one of my clients who was going through a divorce. As we delved into her current struggles, she shared her deepest concern: She noticed a sudden change in her son's behavior. He had become distant, uncommunicative, and even unruly at times. It was a perplexing situation for her as she knew her son to be a good kid at heart.

As we explored the underlying factors, we uncovered a significant missing piece in her son's life—boundaries. In the midst of the divorce and the adjustments that came with it, her son had lost sight of the clear guidelines that used to define their family dynamic. It was crucial to remind him that even in this new chapter, the family rules still applied when he spent time with his mom.

Boundaries are these sacred things that help us inform others what our non-negotiables are. And pretty much every relationship we have in this world is a recognition and respect for each other's boundaries.

My daughter Aarya is a perfect example, being younger to a very strong-willed older sister made her meek as a small kid. She would get bossed all the time. A 4-year-old Aarya one day came crying to me and asked me, "Why do all the kids keep telling me what to do? Everyone always forces me to play the games that I don't want to, why do they not ever listen to me?"

It was a precious moment teaching my little one about drawing boundaries and then guarding them as well. I talked to her about being assertive, about holding her ground and knowing her boundaries. For weeks after that, I heard her implement her version of the lesson. She would respond to the other kids saying, "You are not the boss of me; you have to also listen to me."

Today as a young tween, Aarya has her own personality and interests, and she continues to assert herself. Being a kind soul, she has adapted how she maintains her boundaries. While "you are not the boss of me" is still one of her favorite mantras, I also hear her negotiate, "Let's take turns and do what each of us wants." You will also hear her remind someone when they have stepped over the line of her non-negotiable. She will typically respond with a sarcastic "I forgive you" when she doesn't receive an apology. You see what Aarya is doing is guarding her boundaries, holding them sacred and working diligently to make sure they are known and respected.

I learned my own lesson on boundaries the hard way. We move quite a bit as a consequence of my husband's career. The little town that we were getting posted to did not have many job options for my skill set. I negotiated with my employer to continue working remotely (this was at a time when remote work was not the norm). I felt indebted to my employer for supporting me.

A new manager that I started reporting to realized that I felt indebted and started taking advantage of it. She started by making unkind remarks. If she messaged me and I did not respond right away, she insinuated that I was slacking and taking advantage of my privilege. I would think a million times before taking a bathroom break, or water, or coffee break. Slowly, she continued to step over my boundaries. She would ask me to complete her work for her, saying I can put in some extra hours since I did not have a commute.

I had completely let go of my boundaries. I felt dispirited and embarrassed of how I let myself be taken advantage of. As I decided enough is enough, I took steps to reclaim my space and assert my boundaries. I let her know that I can help her by giving her pointers on her work, but I will not be completing it for her. I let her know that while I will respond to her in a timely manner, I do not appreciate her remarks.

Last but not least, I addressed the issue with the HR team who put in new policies to support work-from-home employees.

I realized that, in an effort to show my gratitude to my employer, I had let go of my boundaries. We often let go of our boundaries in an attempt to show love, kindness, gratitude, compassion. We let the lines blur, and as we do so, we lose our hold on what we hold sacred—our own being. We are taken advantage of, we feel unsupported, and we stop feeling that sense of internal validation as our drivers shift to seek external validation. Moreover, that sense of gratitude and kindness quickly shifts to feelings of anger and resentment.

Why is it important to maintain boundaries?

Boundaries are a way to honor and respect yourself. It is a way to assert your needs and your space. When you set boundaries, you preserve your emotional and spiritual energy. You realize you have the energy and space to be intentional with your time and actions. You also give others around you a clear message that you hold yourself sacred and expect a level of decorum when they deal with you. You become a partner in your relationships with equal power to state and negotiate.

Remember, you learned to draw boundaries from a very young age and you need to keep modifying them as you evolve. Also, it is important to remember that setting boundaries is just 25% of the equation. The remainder 75% of your success hangs on making sure that those around you are aware of your boundaries and respect them. Of course, there will be instances when these will be negotiated, but the negotiation takes place from a place of intention and mutual understanding and respect.

So how do we set our boundaries?

As you step into your own, you will have to go through the effort of understanding your non-negotiables. These could be, among others:

- Topics of discussion
- Tone of voice
- Choice of words
- Type of notice required to plan/do something/be somewhere
- Identifying tasks that you will/will not do

SET BOUNDARIES

Once you have recognized these, identify situations where your boundaries are not firm. These might be areas or topics around which you might feel frustrated or disrespected or unsupported. Make a list of all the things that come to mind and start working diligently to understand. Could there be a boundary that needs to be defined? What is that boundary that you want to define? Who will you need to assert your boundaries to? From here, you need to do the work at re-affirming your boundaries, at speaking up to protect your boundaries and at becoming an active participant in negotiating when needed.

As you start maintaining your boundaries, you will be able to give clear expectations to those around you. This will not only help you to have a better sense of self and better self-esteem, but there will also be less room for conflicts and misunderstandings.

When you have set boundaries, you feel deeply supported and you stop seeking external validation.

Boundaries Exercise

Reflect on Your Boundaries: Take some time to reflect on your own boundaries in different areas of your life, such as relationships, work, and personal well-being. Identify specific areas where you may need to establish or reinforce boundaries. Write down your thoughts and feelings about these boundaries.

_____

_____

_____

_____

Identify Non-Negotiables: Make a list of your non-negotiables—things that are important to you and that you are not willing to compromise on. These could be values, personal needs, or specific limits you want to set. Consider how these non-negotiables align with your current relationships and activities.

_____

_____

_____

_____

SET BOUNDARIES

Communicate Boundaries: Think about how you can effectively communicate your boundaries to others. Practice assertive communication techniques, such as using "I" statements and expressing your needs and expectations clearly. Write down some scenarios where you might need to communicate boundaries, and prepare assertive responses for each situation.

_____

_____

_____

_____

Role-play Boundary Conversations: Enlist a friend or family member to role-play different scenarios where you need to assert your boundaries. Practice expressing your boundaries confidently and responding to potential pushback or negotiation. This exercise can help you feel more prepared and empowered in real-life situations.

_____

_____

_____

_____

Set Boundaries in Small Steps: Start by setting boundaries in small, manageable situations. Practice saying "no" when you genuinely don't want to do something or when it goes against your boundaries. Gradually increase the difficulty level as you become more comfortable with asserting your boundaries.

_____

_____

_____

_____

Remember, setting and maintaining boundaries is a process that takes time and practice. Be patient with yourself and celebrate your progress along the way.

CHAPTER 9

Recharge Your Batteries

*If you want to be truly selfless, recharge your
batteries, for in doing so, you will be able to
spread your light and illuminate more lives*
—Aarti Mehta-Nayyar

DO YOU FEEL drained and exhausted? Do you feel that you are running on fumes but the needs of those around you are so crucial that you can't take time for yourself? You might identify with that feeling where you don't have time to put toward yourself or your passions and hobbies. You always hope to pursue your dreams at a future point in time.

Just as we accept that our devices need to be recharged and cannot run on empty, we must remember that we, too, are energy beings that need recharging.

My maternal grandmother was a deeply selfless woman, someone who made sure everyone came first: her husband, her kids, her grandkids, the extended families, the family pets, the help around the house, the neighbors, the acquaintances, basically everyone came before her. She had the capacity to give beyond all limits, she gave generously of her time, her support, her love, her care, her resources. Everyone spoke of her with love and regard, with utter respect and reverence. It sounds wonderful till I share one of the biggest losses in my life.

As her grandchild, I did not get the entire breadth and depth of that love and attention because she was drained, exhausted, and in ill health by the time I came around. She had given so much of herself and so selflessly that she slipped into poor health at a fairly young age. The lack of attention to her well-being impacted her in later years and she lived her life worried that she was a burden on those she loved.

When I became a mom, I realized one of the most precious experiences my kids can have is the experience of being loved by their grandparents, the experience of going places with them, traveling with them, staying up with them, and building memories. Having lost my paternal grandfather before I was born and my maternal grandfather by the age of 6, I felt a huge vacuum growing up, and my grandmother's ill health added to this vacuum. When I now see my mother following the same pattern of giving selflessly, it hurts me because I know she can't keep giving without recharging.

Just like my selfless grandmother and my mother, I, too, found myself caught in a cycle of giving without considering my own well-being. The realization that I follow this generational pattern came to me when I hit my breaking point.

It was during my husband's deployment as a UN peacekeeper that I truly understood the weight of my self-imposed responsibilities. With two young children (then 3 and 1) and a demanding job, I felt the need to keep everything running as perfectly as it was when my husband was home. It all went well till our nanny left. The unexpected departure of our nanny meant I had to fill the gap while also filling in for my husband and working my full-time job.

These relentless demands and unforeseen circumstances pushed me to my limits. It was when war broke out in the region where my husband was serving that I hit my breaking point. Running on fumes, I had no capacity to handle this additional stress. On the outside, everything looked good. On the inside I was crumbling. I was barely sleeping due to my workload, stress, and anxiety. And finally, the inevitable happened, my body gave way; I was a complete wreck.

My friends had to rush me to the emergency where I was administered a morphine IV to help calm me while my kids were home with other friends. Next morning, I was right where I was the day before: This meant another trip to the emergency room for another round of morphine.

This is when I realized I had to change things and quickly. I was not serving anyone with the way things were unfolding. I was not feeling healthy or happy, and I was not able to show up for my kids while their daddy was away. Things had to change and fast!! I took time off work and focused on my healing and recovery. Slowly, as I cleared my head, I was able to gain some insights and a different perspective. I realized how I needed to break out of the generational pattern I had mechanically slipped into.

I needed to recharge myself to be there for my family. I had to put my needs first and invest in recharging my batteries. The "normalcy" that I was trying to maintain was not what any of us needed. What we needed was to accept the chaos and prioritize the things that would help us stay strong. As I started to get intentional about planning activities that would nourish me as an individual and the three of us, I started to feel capable again, and I was able to take the reins once again. I imagine that this change in attitude not only worked better for myself and the kids but also helped my husband miles away with a sense of relief that we were holding up better and with more grace.

I now have my non-negotiables each day. Little things I do that are just for me and my pleasure, and I deeply cherish these rituals as they fill me up and re-energize me so I can be more present for my loved ones.

Why is it important to recharge?

For someone who has been used to seeking external validation, you might have been conditioned to believe that "selflessness" will get you recognition, appreciation, and the sense of fulfillment you seek. However, as we have discussed, that is not the case. Any recognition you seek and receive will ring untrue unless you are the source of it.

To make sure that you do not fall back in your old ways but instead are moving forward to being your authentic self, you need to actively take time to recharge. In doing so, you fully embody the person who believes in their internal strength and prowess. Also remember, it's only once you are fully recharged you can truly enjoy yourself and be there for your dreams and to support those in your life who you deeply cherish.

So how do you recharge yourself?

To recharge, you have to identify the activities that increase your happiness and your energy level. As you start being mindful, eliminate the energy drainers and replace them with the energizers. Set a time to pursue your energizing interests and invest in them on a daily, weekly, monthly, quarterly, and yearly basis.

Now that we understand the significance of recharging our batteries, let's explore some practical ways to incorporate rejuvenating activities into our lives by seeing some of the examples listed below:

- 20 minutes of reading while enjoying a cup of tea (daily)

- Stretches to release tension from your body (daily)

- Dancing (daily)

- Walking (daily)

- Lunch date with your friends (weekly)
- Pottery class (weekly)
- Watching a musical (monthly)
- Learning a new skill (monthly)
- Going to a retreat (quarterly)
- Sprucing up your wardrobe (quarterly)
- Taking a vacation (bi-annually)
- Reassessing your goals (annually)

As you read through the list and make your own list to recharge, be willing to explore different activities. Be open to adjusting and adapting your routine. Pay attention to what truly brings you joy and make adjustments accordingly. Don›t be afraid to try new activities and experiment with different ways to recharge.

As you start taking time to recharge yourself, you will begin to feel grounded through the day, and you will have more energy to approach life from a state of centeredness. You will have the capacity to help and support others while still being mindful of your own needs. You understand your own importance and your worth not only to yourself but to those around you.

You stop giving of yourself for the sake of external validation and deepen your internal validation.

Daily Activities Exercise

Take a moment to assess how energized or drained you feel on a daily basis. Rate your energy levels on a scale of 1-10 and jot down any patterns or trends you notice.

_____

_____

_____

_____

_____

Make a list of activities that bring you joy, relaxation, and rejuvenation. Refer to the examples mentioned in the chapter or come up with your own. Write down at least five activities that you would like to incorporate into your routine.

_____

_____

_____

_____

_____

RECHARGE YOUR BATTERIES

Choose one or two activities from your list and commit to practicing them daily. Designate specific times during the day when you can engage in these activities and make them non-negotiable.

_____

_____

_____

_____

_____

Select one activity from your list that requires a longer time commitment, such as a monthly pottery class or a quarterly retreat. Schedule these activities in advance and prioritize them as important appointments with yourself.

_____

_____

_____

_____

_____

After practicing your recharge activities for a week or two, reflect on how they have affected your overall well-being. Write down any positive changes you have noticed, such as increased energy, improved mood, or better focus.

_____

_____

_____

_____

Remember, the goal is to prioritize self-care and create a sustainable routine that allows you to recharge regularly. By taking care of yourself, you'll have more to give to others and lead a more fulfilling life.

CHAPTER 10

Understand Your Triggers and Be Prepared

Emotional triggers are reminders nudging us to take our finger off the button. By shifting our reactions, we reclaim control and neutralize their power.
—Aarti Mehta-Nayyar

BY THIS POINT, you should have a stronger sense of internal validation. But are you worried that there are people or events that might trigger you? Most of us have in us the ability to ignore the noise, the naysayers, but there are certain instances when the best of us fail. These instances are great learning opportunities for us to understand our triggers. They reveal to us our unresolved issues, beliefs, hurts, and values that we should have taken the time to acknowledge, learn from, and let go. Know your triggers to know yourself better.

UNDERSTAND YOUR TRIGGERS AND BE PREPARED

I was talking to a client of mine; she is a savvy and successful entrepreneur. As I looked at her, I saw a strong, confident, and sure woman. She was the epitome of a self-made powerhouse. She sat with me and said, "I noticed something and it's really bothering me. I have hired a team of professionals to help me improve my website and vision. It was something I dreamed of—to be big enough and have enough money to hire experts to do a rebrand, a version 2.0 edit of my business and yet I dread them. I am not able to take any feedback. On the contrary I am defensive. I feel like they are attacking me, and I dislike this version of me"

I was touched by her vulnerability. As I talked to her, we discussed her triggers. She said when someone made a suggestion to improve, she took it as an automatic criticism that she did a bad job.

We all have triggers similar to hers. A trigger that I worked through was when someone told me I should manage my house differently.

I would immediately go into a downward spiral, I would feel hurt, judged, and incapable. I would automatically feel I am not competent, like I could just never do anything right. Then next time, I would apply myself with even more fervor to get acknowledgement, even at the cost of my sanity and happiness. The effort I put in taking care of my house no longer came from a place of love; rather, it came from a place of hurt, anger, and unresolved emotions. It wasn't pleasant for me or my family.

Once I realized that I no longer cared for my house from a place of love and rather I did it from a place of anger, I was shocked, I have been gifted with the opportunity to move homes many times over, and I have been blessed to live in beautiful homes each time. I have the joy of each time setting up my belongings to fit the nuances of the new structure that we are going to call home. I have the privilege of sharing that home with my husband and two kids and my family and friends. How could I care for this space with such a strong negative emotion?

I now recognize my trigger, and I no longer get triggered because I have countered my trigger with my facts:

"I have a beautiful home, that my husband and I maintain well.

My home is a safe and nurturing space.

My home is a welcoming space for my family and friends.

If life gets busy, I trust my prioritization of the tasks around the home.

If it does not meet someone's standards, well it is my house and I will respect their decision to meet/stay elsewhere."

Armed with the facts, I know now that if someone judges me for how I manage my house, it is simply their opinion. If I feel it was communicated to me in a manner I do not appreciate, I will have a conversation with them and let them know.

Why do we get triggered and how do we manage our triggers?

We get triggered when we operate from a space of distrust in ourselves and our actions and intentions. If we do not operate from a place of core values and we have been trying too hard to please those around us.

Even despite the best of our efforts, there will be situations where we know as we are walking into them that we are going to be harshly judged. Our ideas or actions will provoke feedback that we are not going to like.

As you build your ability to function from your core, these triggers could set you back, and to avoid any setbacks, it is best to prepare yourself by imagining the incident, the people who will be there, and the reaction you will get. Then prepare a response—the response can range from speaking out to silently observing, to seeing the humor in how well you predicted the reactions.

What do you do when faced with your trigger?

The best way for you to stay empowered when triggered is to prepare as best as you can. Remember, as you practice this state of empowerment more and more, it will become second nature, and you will not have to prepare in advance.

If you can predict the triggering moments you are going to encounter during your day, write them down. As you do so, remind yourself once again why those moments should not trigger you by listing your values, your truths, and your empowered beliefs. Remind yourself on how you are going to maintain your boundaries, and from this place, prepare your response. Depending on who triggers you or the circumstances you might be in, the response may be different.

Below are some of my responses in place for when my trigger shows up:

- I remind myself I know my facts.

- I smile at the person with compassion and forgiveness.

- I remind myself I am living my life on my terms and aligned to my values and nothing else matters.

- I respond back with a polite answer letting the person know they have been unkind and have stepped over my boundary.

Understand your triggers and be prepared. This is your step to let the external world know that you no longer operate from a place of needing external validation.

Learn Your Triggers Exercise

Take some time to reflect and make a list of your triggers. Think about situations or comments that tend to set you off or make you react defensively. Be honest with yourself and write down the triggers that come to mind.

_____

_____

_____

_____

Once you have identified your triggers, explore why they affect you and what underlying beliefs or unresolved issues they might be connected to. Write a paragraph or two for each trigger, delving into the emotions and thoughts that arise when you encounter them.

_____

_____

_____

_____

_____

Choose one of your triggers and reframe it in a more positive and empowering way. For example, if someone criticizing your work triggers you, reframe it as an opportunity for growth and improvement. Write down the new perspective and how it can help you manage the trigger more effectively.

_____

_____

_____

_____

_____

Think about situations where you are likely to encounter your triggers and come up with prepared responses or strategies to handle them. Write down these responses, focusing on assertiveness, empathy, and maintaining your inner peace. Practice saying them aloud to yourself for added confidence.

_____

_____

_____

_____

_____

UNDERSTAND YOUR TRIGGERS AND BE PREPARED

Develop positive affirmations related to your triggers that can help you stay grounded and focused on your self-worth. For example, if someone's judgment triggers you, create an affirmation like, "I am secure in my choices and value myself regardless of others' opinions." Write down your affirmations and repeat them regularly to reinforce positive self-beliefs.

_____

_____

_____

_____

Remember, these exercises are meant to support your personal growth and self-awareness. While you will get better with handling your triggers with time, the goal here is to make sure in the meanwhile you have the tools to prepare yourself.

CHAPTER 11

Build Your Community

Belong by choice, not chance. The right community fuels your growth, turning support into momentum.
—Aarti Mehta-Nayyar

HOW STRONG IS your community? Do you feel safe, supported, and recharged when you are with your community? Do you feel that you can reach out and be heard with love, respect, and understanding?

In human growth and evolution, community has always played a vital role in our species' ability to accomplish more than we can on our own. But not all communities are created equal. Often, we find ourselves part of communities by happenstance—based on inheritance, cultural, or religious beliefs, language, geography and/or a multitude of various factors. We need to realize we have the power to build our community, one that supports us, empowers us, and aligns with our values.

I vividly recall a transformative moment that reshaped my perspective on the power of community. At a personal growth retreat, I found myself surrounded by a diverse group of individuals seeking to better themselves. In one session, we formed small groups and were encouraged to share our deepest fears and insecurities.

As I sat with my newfound community, a mix of vulnerability and apprehension filled the air. However, as each person courageously shared their stories, a remarkable shift occurred. I realized that I was not alone in my struggles. The individuals in my group had similar fears, doubts, and challenges. More importantly, we shared the same drive to break the shackles of our past and become new versions of ourselves. We were all invested in learning and doing the hard work. The empathy, understanding, and support that flowed through that circle of like-minded souls was awe-inspiring. The encouragement to let go and evolve was something I hadn't experienced as powerfully outside of that space.

This experience made me realize the profound importance of surrounding myself with a community where I found resonance. A community where our belonging went beyond surface level conversations, where we could engage at a level of depth and vulnerability that reflected the significance of our relationships. I no longer desired to be part of circles that fueled gossip and judgment. Instead, I sought a community that empathized with the tough parts of our journeys, cheered one another on, and celebrated our collective accomplishments.

Through the power of digital connection, I discovered an online tribe of like-minded individuals who shared a common desire to grow, evolve, and contribute to the world. Today, I feel deeply connected, knowing that I have a safety net that has my emotional back and will always push me forward when I stumble.

As you embark on your journey as a self-aware being, I urge you to take a closer look at your community and consider whether you can build or find a better one. Do you have enough community around you that enables your recently discovered self to fully express?

The digital age has provided us with unprecedented opportunities to connect with people who align with our values, experiences, and challenges. You can intentionally seek out communities that resonate with your authentic self. Being part of a community that fits your new persona will foster your growth and evolution in ways you never thought possible. It will serve as a check to prevent you from falling back into old habits, and it will empower you to live unapologetically.

Building your community is an ongoing process. It may take time to find the right connections and cultivate meaningful relationships. Stay open-minded, be authentic, and focus on creating a supportive and empowering community that helps you thrive.

Remember, your community has the power to shape your growth and influence your perspective. Just as I discovered during that transformative retreat, surrounding yourself with a tribe of individuals who understand, uplift, and celebrate you can be truly transformative. Together, we can forge a community that fuels our collective evolution, propelling us toward lives of purpose, fulfillment, and genuine connection.

As you become part of a community of like-minded individuals, your internal validation will get further fueled.

Build Your Community Exercise

Think about the people you interact with regularly, both offline and online. Consider your friends, family, colleagues, social groups, and online communities. Ask yourself the following questions:

Do you feel supported, safe, and understood in your current communities?

_____

_____

_____

Do your communities align with your values and aspirations?

_____

_____

_____

Are there any toxic or negative influences in your communities that hold you back or drain your energy?

_____

_____

_____

Are there any gaps in your community where you desire more connection and support?

_____

_____

_____

Imagine your ideal community, one that aligns with your authentic self and supports your personal growth and well-being. Think about the qualities, values, and characteristics you would like to see in your ideal community. Consider the types of relationships, conversations, and support that would be present.

_____

_____

_____

_____

Take action to build your community: Based on your reflection, identify steps you can take to build or enhance your community. Consider the following actions:

Seek out new communities: Explore online platforms, social groups, clubs, or organizations that align with your interests, values, or goals. Join communities where you can connect with like-minded individuals and engage in meaningful discussions.

Invest time and effort in nurturing relationships with people who are supportive, understanding, and aligned with your values. Foster deeper connections by having open and honest conversations, sharing experiences, and supporting each other's growth.

Evaluate the relationships in your current community and establish healthy boundaries with toxic or negative influences. Surround yourself with people who uplift and inspire you, while distancing yourself from those who drain your energy or hinder your personal growth.

Consistently assess the quality of your current communities and take proactive steps to build a community that aligns with your personal growth and well-being. One that celebrates your uniqueness and motivates you to be your authentic self.

UNSTOPPABLE YOU

WELCOME, UNSTOPPABLE YOU. It is my pleasure and deepest honor to be one of the first ones to welcome this version of you.

Let me remind you of the journey we have shared and how far you have come:

1. You took the time to get to know yourself better, to connect with your soul, your uniqueness and what makes you, YOU—the perfect fit for this beautiful planet. The expression of you that is paramount for you, your loved ones, and for humankind.

2. Next, you went on to honor yourself. To understand you need nurturing, you need care, and you need acknowledgement and time to be your truest version. To truly understand that your ability to care and love should be first practiced on yourself before you can share it with others.

3. Finally, you stepped into your power with kindness and firmness, letting the world know that you will share your space but not cramp it

to accommodate others. You have made clear that you are as deserving of respect and understanding as every other person out there.

At this point, with all the work you have put in, you can be nothing but unstoppable, living your life with self-validation.

Living a life rooted in self-validation while maintaining humility, kindness, compassion, and empathy is a profound gift you can give to yourself. It elevates your being and allows you to fully savor and evolve in every aspect of your life.

From this place of abundance and self-approval, external validation loses its grip on you. No longer are you driven by the opinions and expectations of others. Instead, you hold yourself to higher values and live life on your own terms.

Remember, self-validation is a skill that requires conscious practice. Just like we consistently work out to strengthen our physical muscles, it is essential to revisit the exercises and insights shared in this book. I encourage you to continue practicing the principles you have uncovered and return to this book whenever you need a reminder or seek new areas of self-appreciation and acknowledgment.

If you stumble or falter along the way, show compassion to yourself. Take the time to be with yourself, recharge your inner energy, set and protect your boundaries, understand your triggers, and reach out to your community for support. If there are lingering negative emotions toward someone, embrace forgiveness and let go. And above all, acknowledge and honor yourself. Recognize that your soul is here to savor the human experience and contribute to making the world a better place.

So what does living with self-validation look like for you?

It means becoming more confident in yourself, gaining clarity on the direction you want to navigate in life, embracing both your perfections and imperfections, finding deep satisfaction, and ceasing to compare yourself to others, rather recognizing your unique growth opportunities and investing in them to live a life fully expressed. It means being unapologetic for the choices you make, cultivating calmness and serenity even in the midst of chaos, prioritizing your health and well-being, having more time for the things you enjoy, and ultimately living life on your own terms. This is how fulfillment blossoms.

Does living with self-validation imply that you won't encounter hardships?

Not at all. Life will inevitably throw challenges your way. However, by nurturing self-validation, you will have built a rock-solid foundation that empowers you to bounce back resiliently. By mastering self-validation, you transform tough times from personal failures or concerns about others' opinions into opportunities for growth, acceptance, and transformation.

Now that I am unstoppable, what's next?

Now that you have unleashed this unstoppable version of yourself, I invite you to rekindle those dreams and desires that you may have put on hold, see if they still excite you, be courageous to dream new dreams, be playful, be curious, and explore what sparks joy in you and calls on you. If you are interested, head over to my website and sign up for my free live workshop—The Next Horizon.

I extend my heartfelt wishes for your success. May you live a life guided by your inner truth, and may your self-validation empower you to create a world of joy, fulfillment, and authenticity.

Stay connected as you progress through your journey and share your success stories as you Stop Seeking external validation and Start Being your true authentic self.

GLOSSARY

1. **Boundaries** - Boundaries are the invisible lines we draw to protect our energy, time, and well-being. They define what we allow into our lives and what we respectfully decline, honoring our needs and values in every interaction. True boundaries aren't walls; they are compassionate guidelines that support our relationships and personal growth, ensuring we stay true to ourselves while engaging meaningfully with others.

2. **Compassion** - Compassion is the gentle, expansive energy that allows us to see others—and ourselves—through a lens of understanding, kindness, and empathy. It's the recognition that we are all imperfect and that our shared humanity binds us in our struggles and joys. True compassion requires no judgment; it is the willingness to hold space for others' journeys while nurturing our own. Through compassion, we learn to release anger and resentment, creating a bridge between forgiveness and inner peace.

3. **Core Values** - Core values are the unwavering beliefs that guide us, the essence of who we are

beneath the layers of expectation and external influence. They are the principles that give shape to our choices and our character, aligning our actions with our authentic selves. Knowing and living by our core values is a form of self-respect; it is the path to living a life that feels deeply fulfilling and true.

4. **Emotional Triggers** - Emotional triggers are the moments that stir strong reactions within us, often tapping into past experiences, fears, or unresolved emotions. They are like signals, inviting us to pause and reflect rather than react impulsively. By understanding our triggers, we regain control over our responses, transforming these reminders into opportunities for growth and self-awareness.

5. **Enoughness** - Enoughness is the quiet assurance that who you are, right here, and right now, is already whole and worthy. It is the release of comparison and the embrace of self-acceptance, a recognition that you do not need to prove your value to anyone—including yourself. Living in a state of enoughness allows you to pursue growth from a place of joy, rather than lack, and to see yourself as complete, with every flaw and strength alike.

6. **Growth Edge** - A growth edge is the place within us where comfort meets challenge, where we are called to step out of the familiar and embrace the unknown for the sake of our evolution. It's the

point at which we can lean into discomfort with trust, knowing that each step forward expands our resilience, our knowledge, and our capacity to live fully. The growth edge invites us to see not only who we are, but who we are capable of becoming.

7. **Hero's Journey** - Almost every trial or tough time that we have gone through gives us the opportunity to describe how we came out the other end. We get an opportunity to shine light on our strengths and lessons learned. This narrative is about the courageous pursuit of growth, where challenges become teachers, and every setback becomes part of our personal evolution. This narrative is the hero's journey, and embracing it means seeing ourselves not as victims of circumstance but as active participants in our story, empowered by every experience that shapes us.

8. **Hindsight Window** - The hindsight window is the compassionate lens through which we revisit our past, allowing us to see our former selves with understanding rather than judgment. By adjusting this window, we learn to honor the choices and challenges of who we once were, recognizing growth and wisdom gained over time. A clear hindsight window empowers us to release regret, accept past experiences, and use them as stepping stones toward a more resilient and empowered self.

9. **Imposter Syndrome** - Imposter syndrome is the persistent feeling that we are somehow not

deserving of our achievements, that we are 'faking it' despite evidence of our abilities. It's the quiet doubt that creeps in, making us question our worth and competency. Understanding imposter syndrome allows us to see it for what it is—a mental barrier, not a truth. Overcoming it involves trusting in our journey, owning our successes, and allowing ourselves to feel worthy of every accomplishment

10. **Internal Validation** - Recognition that true fulfillment comes from within. It is the steady assurance that our thoughts, feelings, and achievements are valid without needing external praise. By grounding ourselves in internal validation, we build a foundation of self-trust and authenticity, allowing us to navigate life with a sense of wholeness and inner peace.

11. **Negative Spiral** - A negative spiral is the cycle of self-doubt or discouragement that can arise from repeated criticism, unmet expectations, or lingering insecurities. It's a pattern that feeds on itself, often clouding our perception of our true worth. Recognizing a negative spiral empowers us to break free from its grip, shifting our focus from self-criticism to self-compassion, and reestablishing a positive, empowering mindset.

12. **People-pleaser** - A people-pleaser is someone who habitually prioritizes others' needs and desires, often at the expense of their own well-being. While the intentions may come

from a place of kindness, this behavior can lead to burnout and self-neglect. Breaking free from people-pleasing means embracing self-respect and setting boundaries that honor both our own needs and the relationships we value.

13. **Self-awareness** - Self-awareness is the conscious exploration of who we are beneath the surface—our values, triggers, strengths, and areas for growth. It is the journey of understanding ourselves deeply so we can make intentional choices that align with our true essence. With self-awareness, we gain clarity on our path and compassion for our process.

14. **Self-compassion** - The gentle act of treating ourselves with the same kindness, patience, and understanding that we extend to others. It is the ability to forgive our own missteps and to hold space for our imperfections without judgment. Practicing self-compassion allows us to nurture our resilience and strengthens our capacity for growth

15. **Self-validation** - Self-validation is the practice of affirming our own worth, acknowledging our thoughts, feelings, and achievements without relying on external approval. It is the gentle assurance that we are enough, rooted in our values and experiences. Self-validation frees us from the need for others' approval, allowing us to live in alignment with our own truth and to honor our unique journey with confidence.

GLOSSARY

16. **Self-worth** - That unshakable belief in our own value, a deep understanding that we are deserving of love, respect, and kindness simply by being ourselves. It's not determined by accomplishments or approval; it is an intrinsic quality that resides within. Cultivating self-worth is the act of honoring ourselves fully, imperfections and all.

17. **Victim Mindset** - Sometimes as we go through experiences, we get too attached to the story and how it impacted us. We see ourselves as victims that were let down/hurt/abandoned. If we take on this thinking often enough, we begin to build a victim mindset. Rhis is where we consistently feel that we are alone, unsupported, or feel like life is happening to us, rather than through us. This is an extremely disempowered state to be in as it keeps us from seeing our strengths, thus leading to disempowerment and a loss of self-confidence

ABOUT THE AUTHOR

AARTI'S JOURNEY BEGAN with a familiar feeling: the shrinking of joy and fulfillment in life as she tirelessly tried to please others. No matter how much she gave of herself, true recognition and celebration seemed always just out of reach. This cycle led her to a pivotal realization: True freedom and happiness come from self-validation, not from seeking approval.

Determined to break free, Aarti embarked on a transformative journey that empowered her to embrace her own worth. This experience ignited a desire to help others find the same freedom. She knew that millions were still trapped in similar patterns, and she was committed to guiding them toward a life of self-respect, authenticity, and fulfillment.

Today, Aarti is a corporate and personal coach, helping people-pleasers and high performers alike tap into their fullest potential. With a background in building stronger team cultures and boosting productivity, she blends her insights on soft skills, continuous improvement, and self-validation to inspire and uplift her clients. Through her programs, Aarti helps individuals and teams move from simply "getting by" to becoming unstoppable.

ABOUT THE AUTHOR

When she isn't coaching, writing, or speaking, Aarti connects with her readers and community on Instagram as @coachaarti and through her website, www.coachaarti.com. Her mission is clear: to empower others to step into their power, shed the habit of people-pleasing, and discover the freedom of self-validation.

www.ingramcontent.com/pod-product-compliance
Lightning Source LLC
Chambersburg PA
CBHW060802050426
42449CB00008B/1487